CHAS & DAVE
SONGBOOK

CHAS & DAVE

www.chasndave.com

© 2008 by Faber Music Ltd
First published by Faber Music Ltd in 2008
Bloomsbury House
74–77 Great Russell Street
London WC1B 3DA

Arranged by Olly Weeks
Edited by Lucy Holliday & Alex Davis

Designed by Lydia Merrills-Ashcroft
Photographs courtesy of Chas & Dave
Cover Photograph by Richard Skidmore

Printed in England by Caligraving Ltd
All rights reserved

ISBN10: 0-571-53134-2
EAN13: 978-0-571-53134-9

Reproducing this music in any form is illegal and forbidden
by the Copyright, Designs and Patents Act, 1988

To buy Faber Music publications or to find out about the full range of titles available,
please contact your local music retailer or Faber Music sales enquiries:

Faber Music Ltd, Burnt Mill, Elizabeth Way, Harlow, CM20 2HX England
Tel: +44(0)1279 82 89 82   Fax: +44(0)1279 82 89 83
sales@fabermusic.com   fabermusicstore.com

AIN'T NO PLEASING YOU 08
BEER BELLY 14
THE DIDDLUM SONG 17
FLYING 22
GERTCHA 30
HARRY WAS A CHAMPION 36
I WONDER IN WHOSE ARMS 42
IN SICKNESS AND IN HEALTH 49
LONDON GIRLS 52
MARGATE 56
MUSTN'T GRUMBLE 61
ONE OF THEM DAYS 64
POOR OLD MR WOOGIE 68
RABBIT 72
THE SIDEBOARD SONG 76
SNOOKER LOOPY 82
THAT OLD PIANO 86
THAT'S WHAT I LIKE 91
WALLOP 100
WISH I COULD WRITE A LOVE SONG 96

Bonus Piano Solo
FLYING 27

Biography

In the tradition of The Kinks and the Small Faces and around the same time as Ian Dury and Squeeze, Chas & Dave wrote and recorded exceptionally witty songs about life in London, performed with a strong affection for all things English reminiscent of many of the great Music Hall artists many years previously. In their case, however, the musical accompaniment to their sharply observant material was neither rock nor punk but solid, no-nonsense Rock'N'Roll style which had been their background and inspiration.

Pianist **Chas Hodges** and guitarist **Dave Peacock** were widely experienced around the British rock scene of the 1960s and early 70s before teaming up with drummer **Mick Burt** (another much-travelled musician who had gone back to his original trade as a plumber) to form the group. Chas had worked with the legendary producer **Joe Meek**, backed **Jerry Lee Lewis**, played with **Mike Berry and the Outlaws**, along with **Ritchie Blackmore**, and also the highly respected Cliff Bennett and the Rebel Rousers, which had Burt on drums. He then joined **Albert Lee's** cult band **Heads Hands and Feet** before playing with Dave and Albert in Black Claw. Dave had been equally active, Starting out in The Rolling Stones (no, not them!) in 1960. Spells with **The Tumbleweeds**, **Mick Greenwood**, **Jerry Donaghue**, and the above mentioned Black Claw followed prior to the pair coming together to go out on their own as Chas & Dave.

Their debut album 'One Fing 'n' Anuvver' was released on the Retreat label in 1975 earning critical acclaim from the likes of John Peel among others. This self-produced offering was perhaps the first (definitely the strongest) example of cockney Rock 'n' Roll, with song titles such as 'Ponders End Allotments Club' giving a strong North London angle to the genre. Their proudly cockney vocals and exuberant good humour, blended with their love for genuine Rock'n'Roll, led them to title their 1978 EMI album 'Rockney' (later to become their label name) which featured some top quality songwriting and was championed, before their commercial success, by the influential DJ Charlie Gillett. Two years later they were spotted by an advertising exec at a pub gig playing their composition 'Gertcha'; he signed them up to make ads for Courage beer and lucrative popularity naturally resulted as well as awards for the ads themselves. 'Gertcha' became their first Top Twenty chart entry. They followed up with 'The Sideboard Song (Got my Beer in The Sideboard Here)' from their third album 'Don't Give A Monkey's', and their two most successful singles, 1980's 'Rabbit' (from the same album) and the fine, more reflective ballad 'Ain't No Pleasing You' two years later. In between they recorded their first live album - 'Live At Abbey Road' - for EMI. The famous Studio One being converted into an East end pub for the occasion with friends and industry invited.

More popular recordings came along with 'Margate' and 'London Girls' and a move into the sporting world, collaborating with the Matchroom Mob on 'Snooker Loopy' in 1986, and Tottenham Hotspur FC on their FA cup final songs. The 80s also saw Christmas releases with collections of their favourite old time songs brought back for a new audience. The boys still found time to contribute theme tunes for TV shows such as 'Crackerjack' and 'In Sickness & In Health'. Regular appearances on our screens as well as their own TV specials boosted their profile to household name status. Perhaps the high point of the decade though was being presented with the 'Red Book' by **Eamonn Andrews** on the TV show 'This Is Your Life' during the show's heyday in 1985.

Throughout the 90s they switched their attention to new projects. They worked with the late **Johnny Speight** - creator of Alf Garnett. And they recorded a collection of songs to commemorate the 50th anniversary of V.E day in 1995. This proved to be their most successful album to date hitting number two in the charts (kept off of the top spot only by Take That's farewell album). The accompanying video was equally successful. In 1998 they had an unexpected breakthrough in America when radio stations started playing their track 'Flying' in heavy rotation, resulting in overwhelming public response. This lead to them being snapped up by US label Cleveland International and 'The World Of Chas & Dave' album was released to cash in on the buzz, which it duly did, winning them scores of fans in the states including **Jack Clement**, legendary engineer at Sun Studios (who is credited as having discovered Jerry Lee Lewis no less). So 25 years on, the boys found themselves touring the US for the first time.

In this new century, Chas & Dave's appeal has never been greater or more varied. The audiences are getting younger without the boys deliberately trying to appeal to the youth, and new bands are citing them as a major influence. None more so than **The Libertines**, who when asked who they wanted on the bill with them on their London shows in 2003/2004, didn't hesitate... Chas & Dave. The shows at The Brixton Academy & The Kentish Town Forum were a huge success with Pete & Carl from the band joining Chas & Dave on stage for a couple of numbers. This glowing endorsement from the band of the moment opened a lot of people's eyes and ears to Chas & Dave.

In 2005 Chas & Dave joined forces with EMI once more resulting in two top selling CD releases. The year also saw their long overdue debut at the Glastonbury Festival as they packed out the acoustic stage with over thirty thousand fans singing along. The year ended on a high with a sold out christmas beano at the Shepherd's Bush empire which was filmed by EMI for a debut DVD release.

AIN'T NO PLEASING YOU

Words and Music by Charles Hodges and David Peacock

© 1982 Snout Music Ltd

BEER BELLY
Words and Music by Charles Hodges and David Peacock

© 1981 Snout Music Ltd

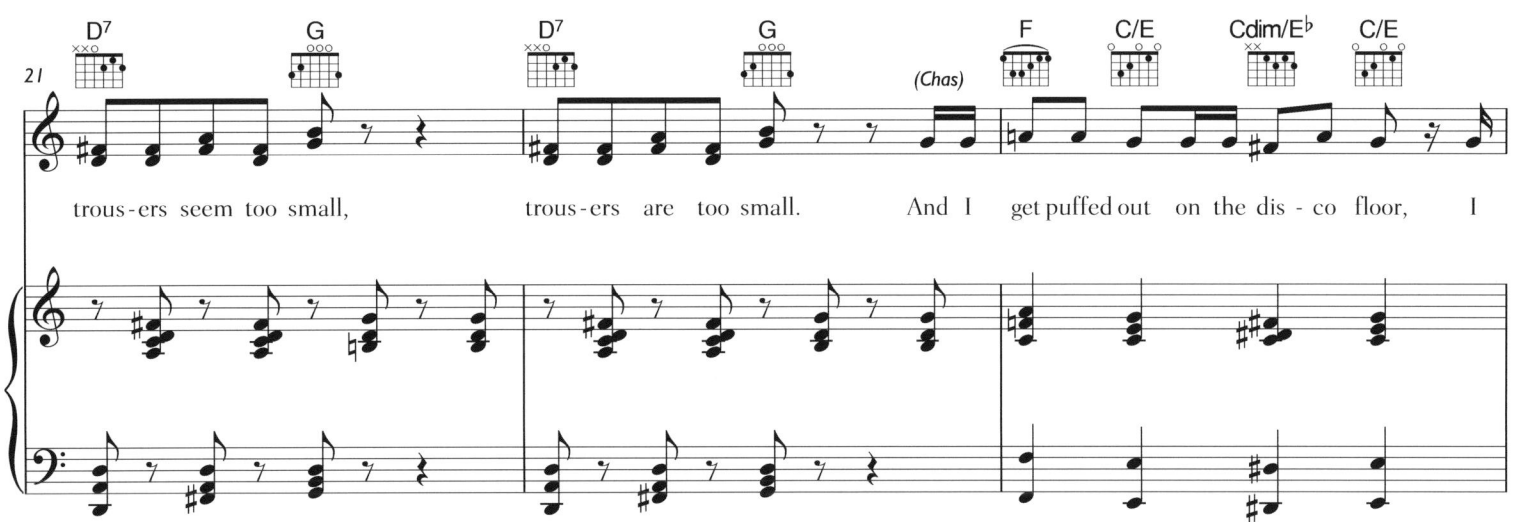

THE DIDDLUM SONG
Words and Music by Charles Hodges and David Peacock

© 1987 Snout Music Ltd

FLYING

Words and Music by Charles Hodges and David Peacock

© 1987 Snout Music Ltd

FLYING
(piano solo)
Words and Music by Charles Hodges and David Peacock

© 1987 Snout Music Ltd

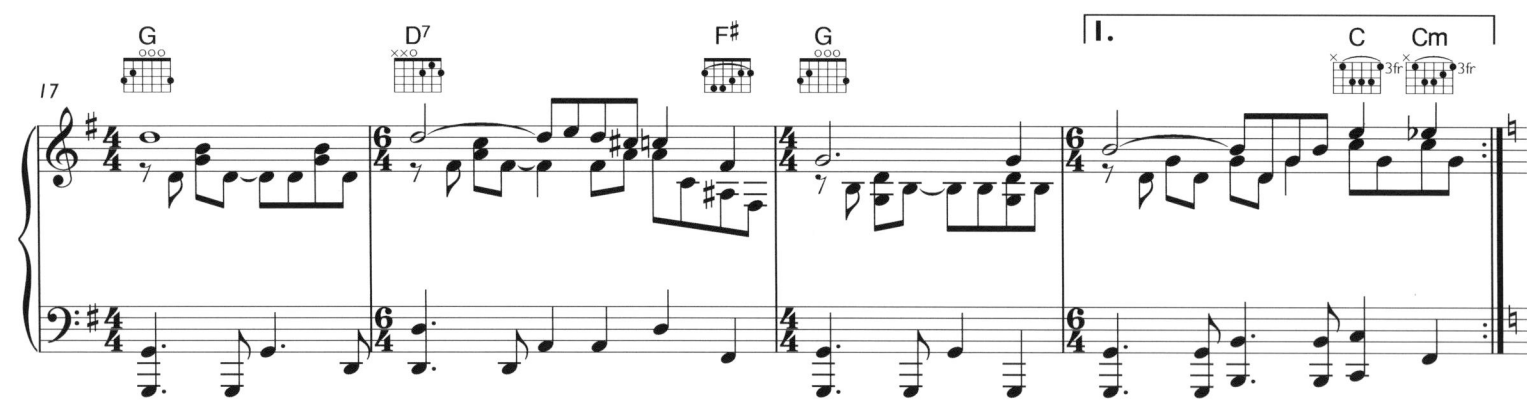

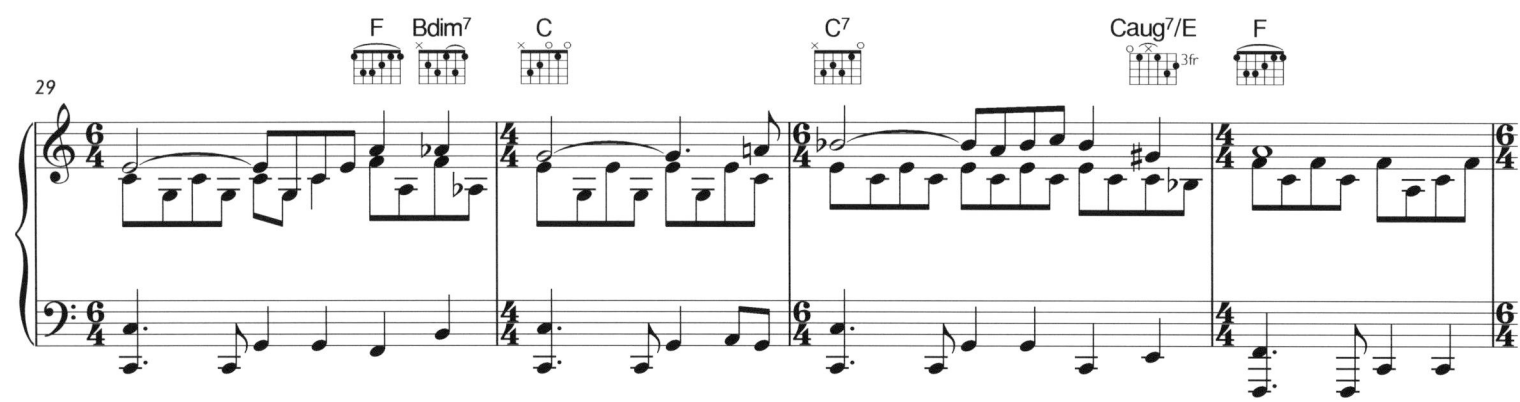

GERTCHA
Words and Music by Charles Hodges and David Peacock

© 1979 Snout Music Ltd and Big Jim Music
Snout Music Ltd and EMI Music Publishing Ltd

HARRY WAS A CHAMPION
Words and Music by Charles Hodges and David Peacock

© 1984 Snout Music Ltd

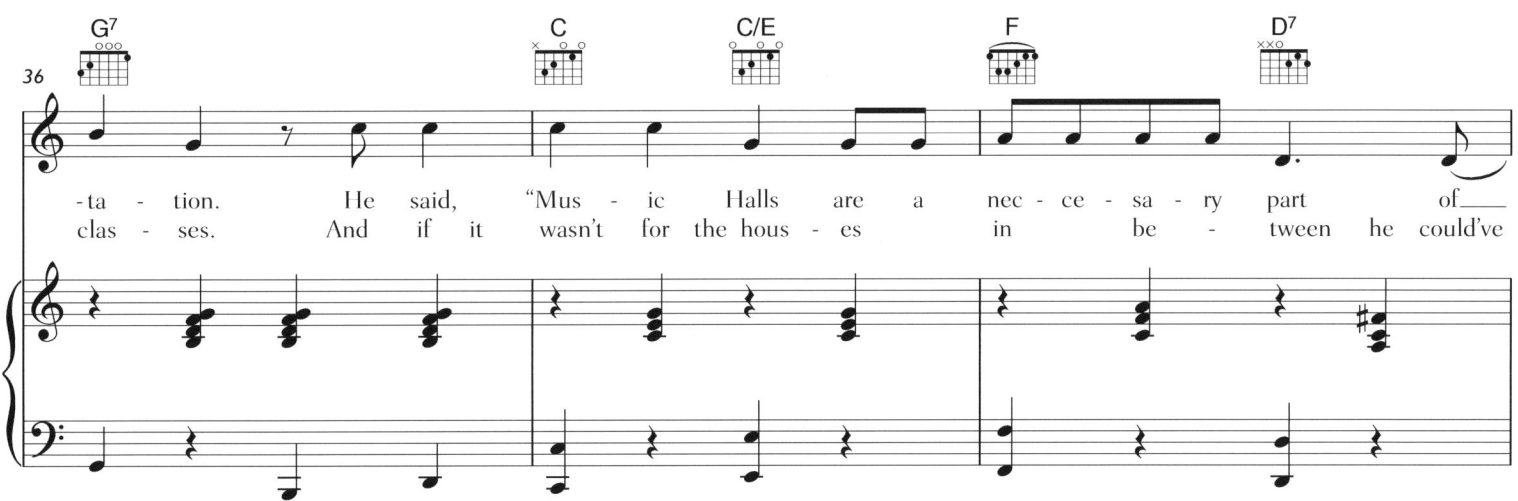
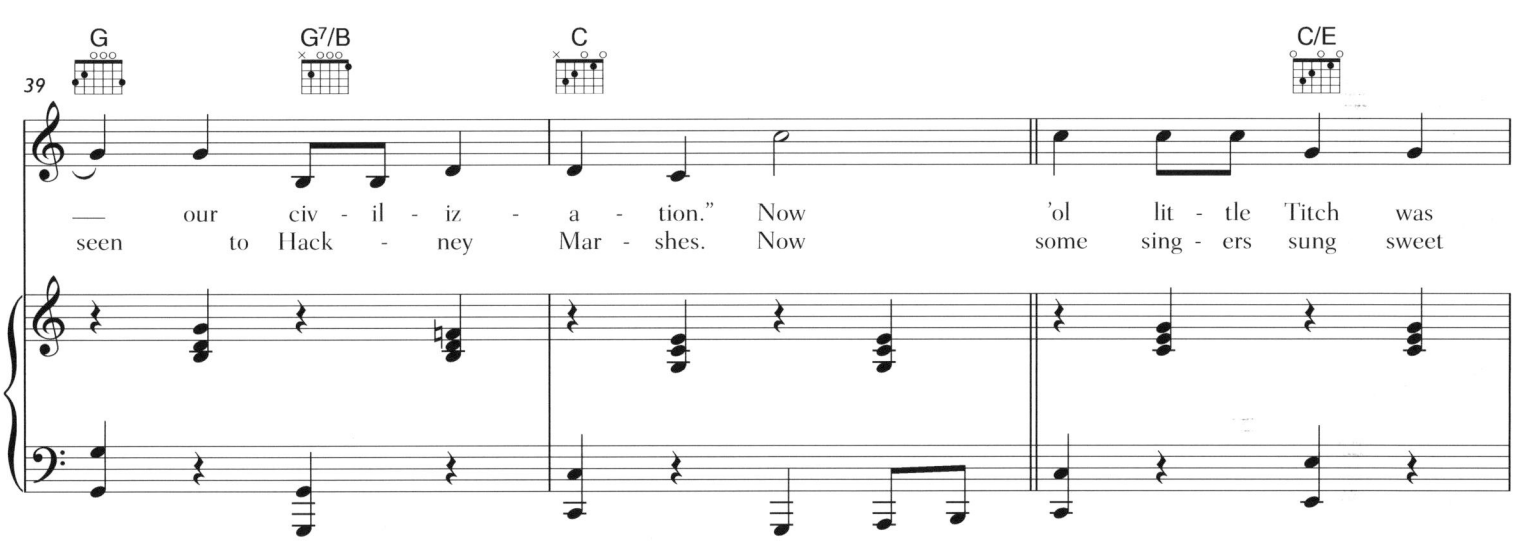
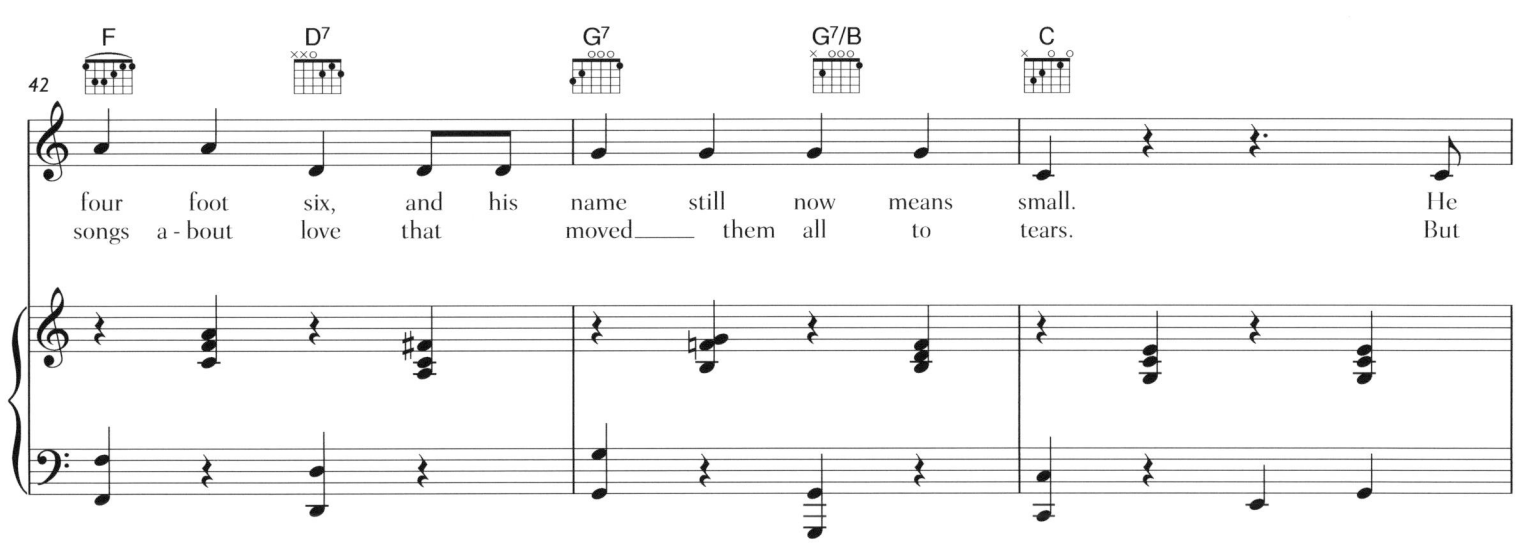

I WONDER IN WHOSE ARMS
Words and Music by Charles Hodges and David Peacock

© 1984 Snout Music Ltd

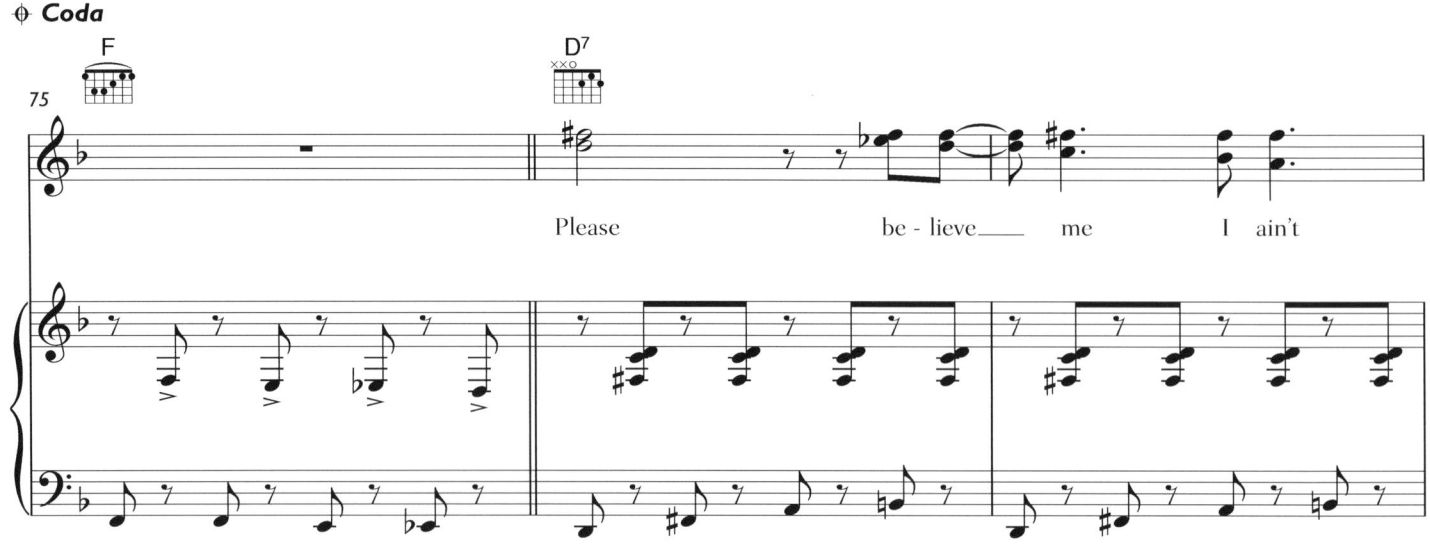

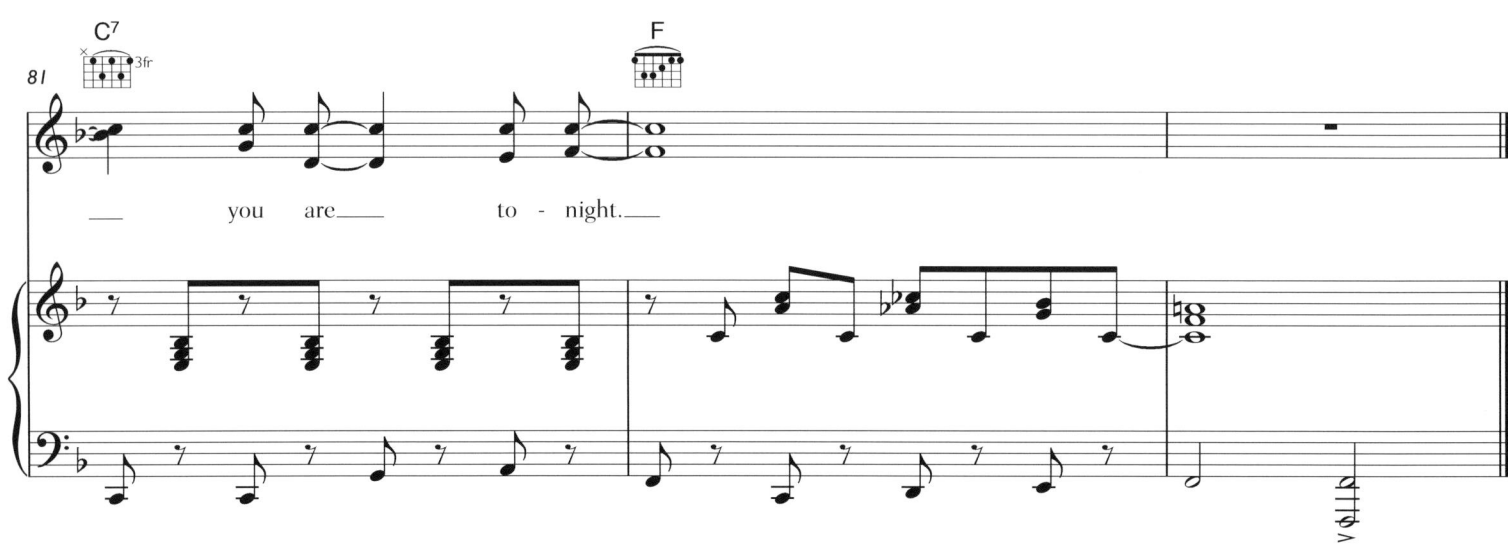

IN SICKNESS AND IN HEALTH
Words and Music by Charles Hodges and David Peacock

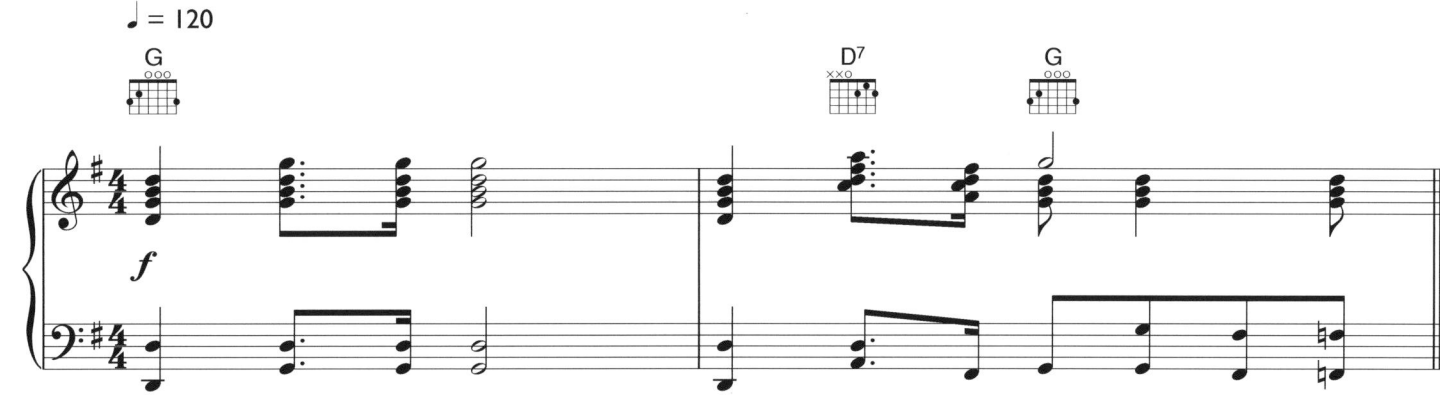

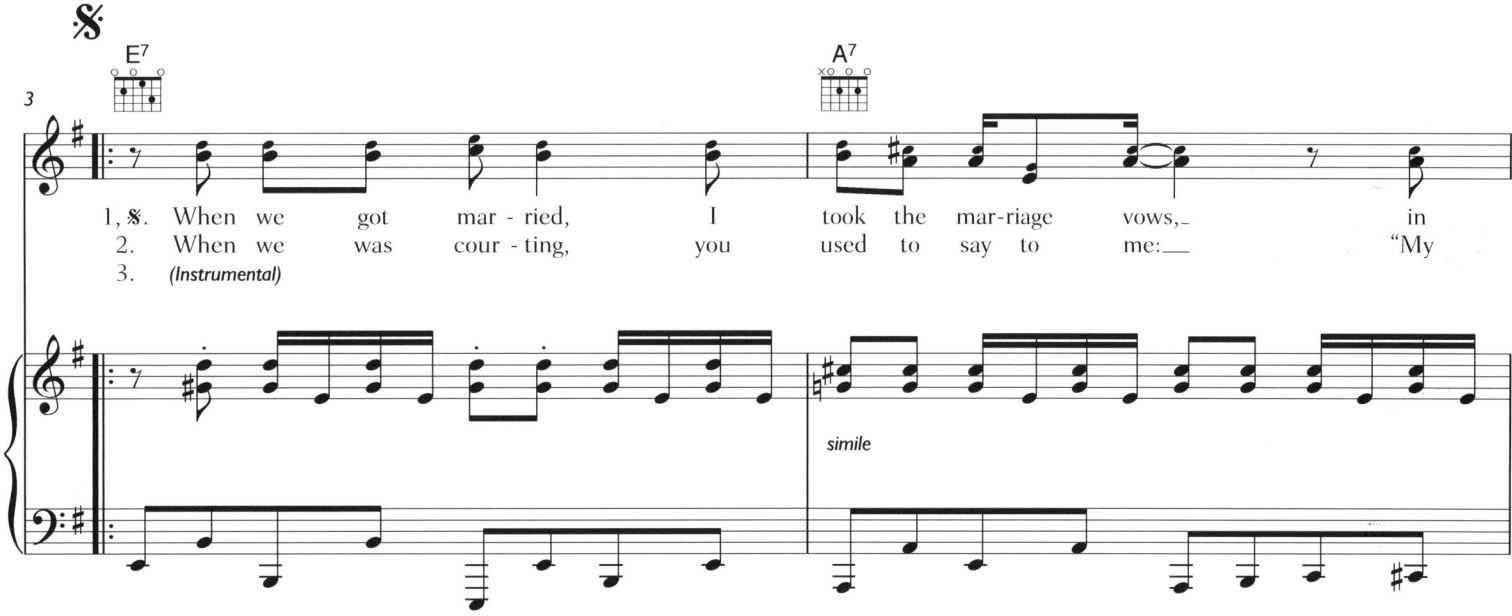

1., %. When we got mar - ried, I took the mar - riage vows,_ in
2. When we was cour - ting, you used to say to me:_ "My
3. *(Instrumental)*

sick - ness and in health I said: "I do", for
dar - ling, I can't wait_ un - til we're wed. I'll

© 1985 Snout Music Ltd

LONDON GIRLS

Words and Music by Charles Hodges and David Peacock

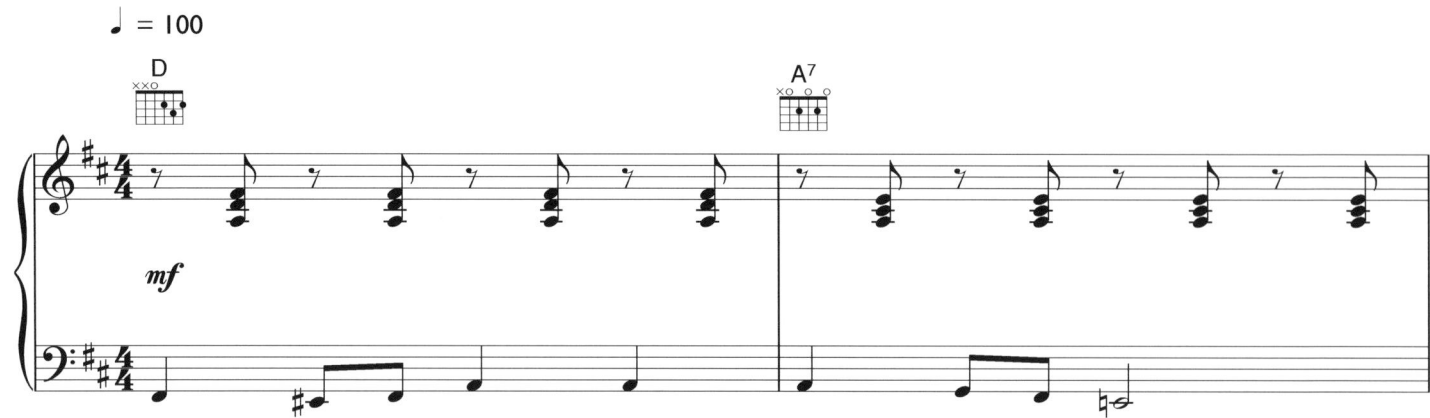

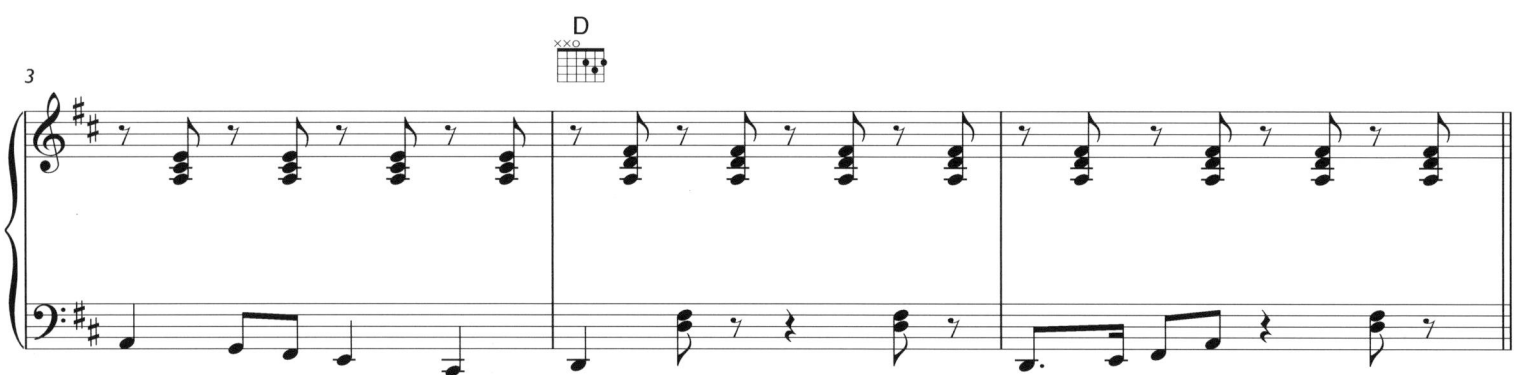

1. Some peo-ple sing a-bout Deut-sche girls___ and girls from Ca-li-for-nia, they
2. Mar-ry a girl from Lon-don Town___ you know you can trust 'em, they'll
3. Lon-don___ girls are the best in the world, there ain't no doubt a-bout___ it, if you
(4.) ever go down to Lon-don Town___ your legs will turn to jel-ly, 'cos the

© 1983 Snout Music Ltd

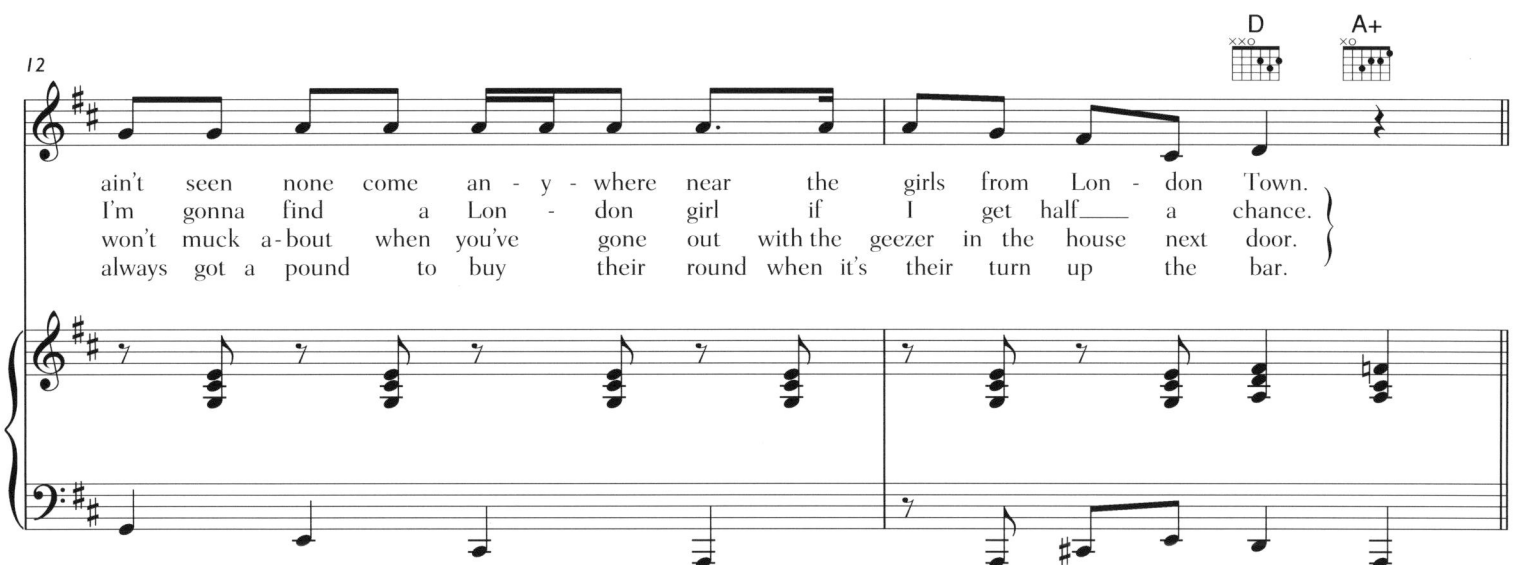

MARGATE
Words and Music by Charles Hodges and David Peacock

© 1982 Snout Music Ltd

MUSTN'T GRUMBLE
Words and Music by Charles Hodges and David Peacock

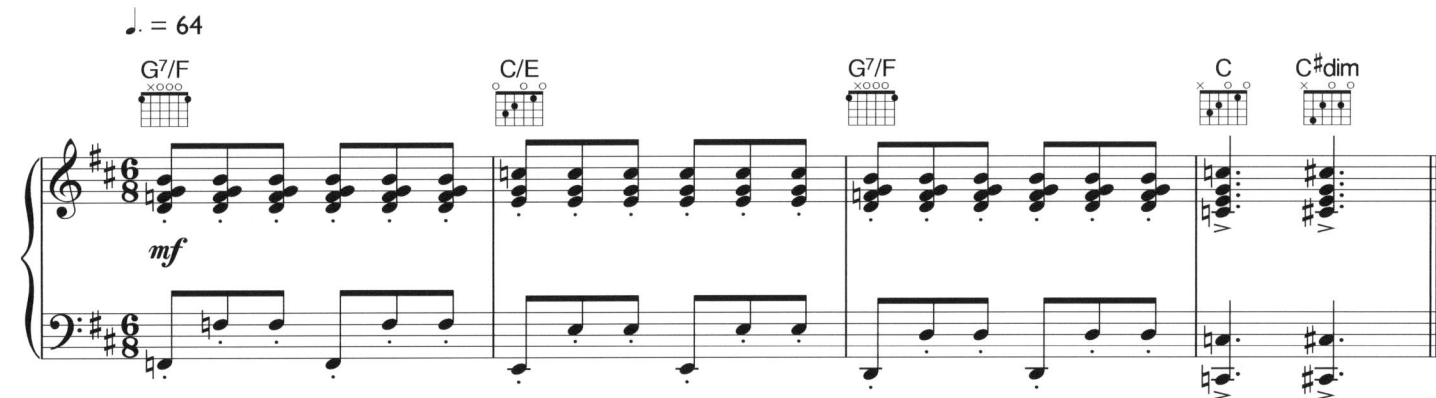

1, 5. Now I

(1.) had an old un-cle as mean as can be, he said: "When I die you'll get
2. All he left me was an old ov-er-coat, but I found in the pocket a
(3.) I am a "do it your-self-er", you see, it can half make life eas-y,
(4.) wife wants the grass cut or a new kit-chen shelf, just do as I do and say:
(5.) came home from work, there was fire-men a-round, they said: "We could-n't save it, your
(6.) said: "That's al-right, don't wor-ry mate, 'cos the bath-room needed paint-ing, it weren't
7. I collect the foot-ball pools mon-ey, you see, and one week we won it, my
8. I went home ear-ly feeling pleased with me-self, then I saw the coup-on still

© 1981 Snout Music Ltd

ONE OF THEM DAYS

Words and Music by Charles Hodges and David Peacock

© 1984 Snout Music Ltd

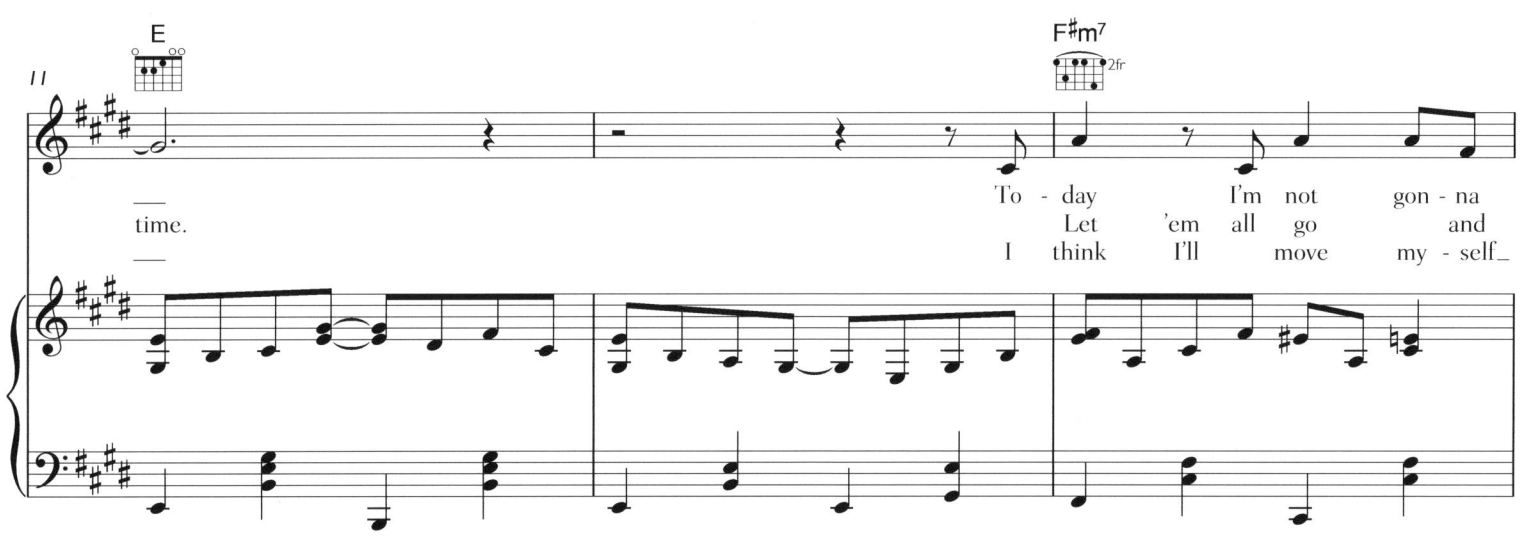
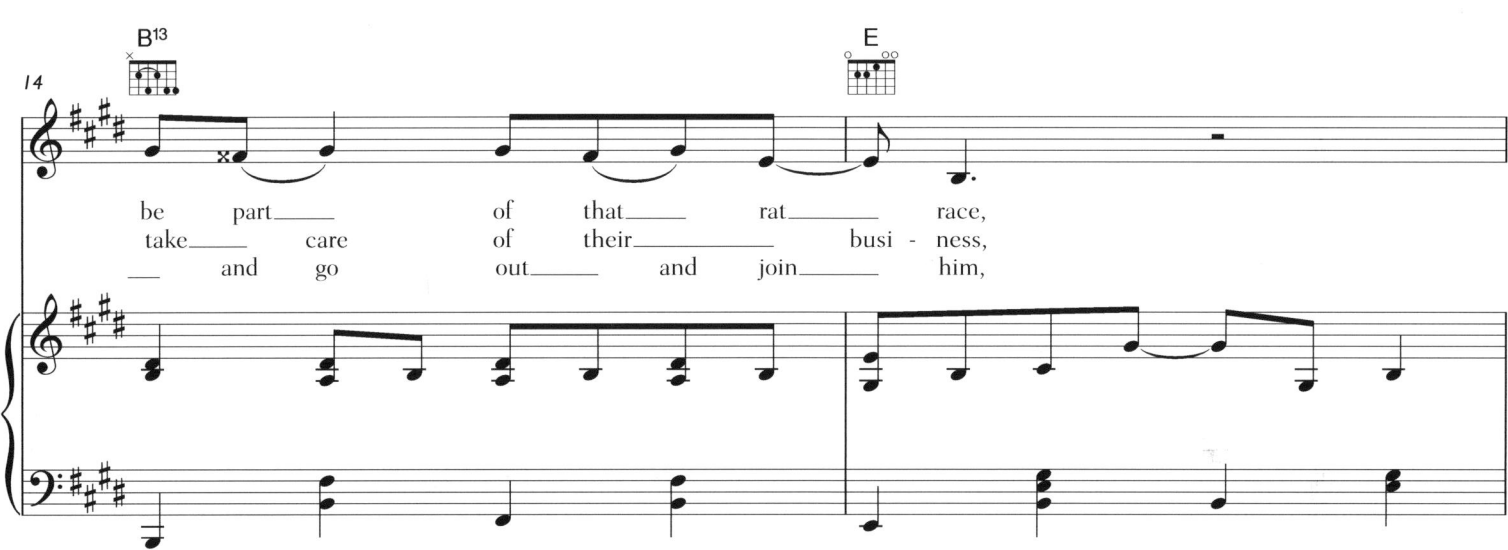

POOR OLD MR WOOGIE

Words and Music by Charles Hodges and David Peacock

© 1981 Snout Music Ltd

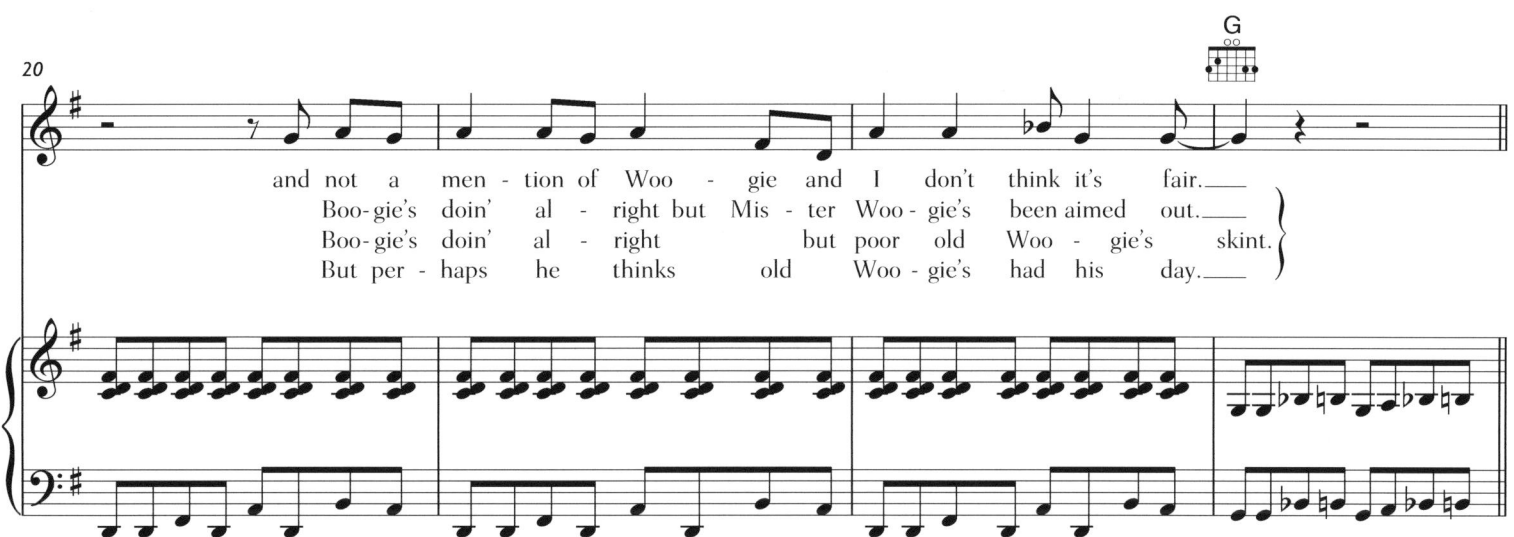

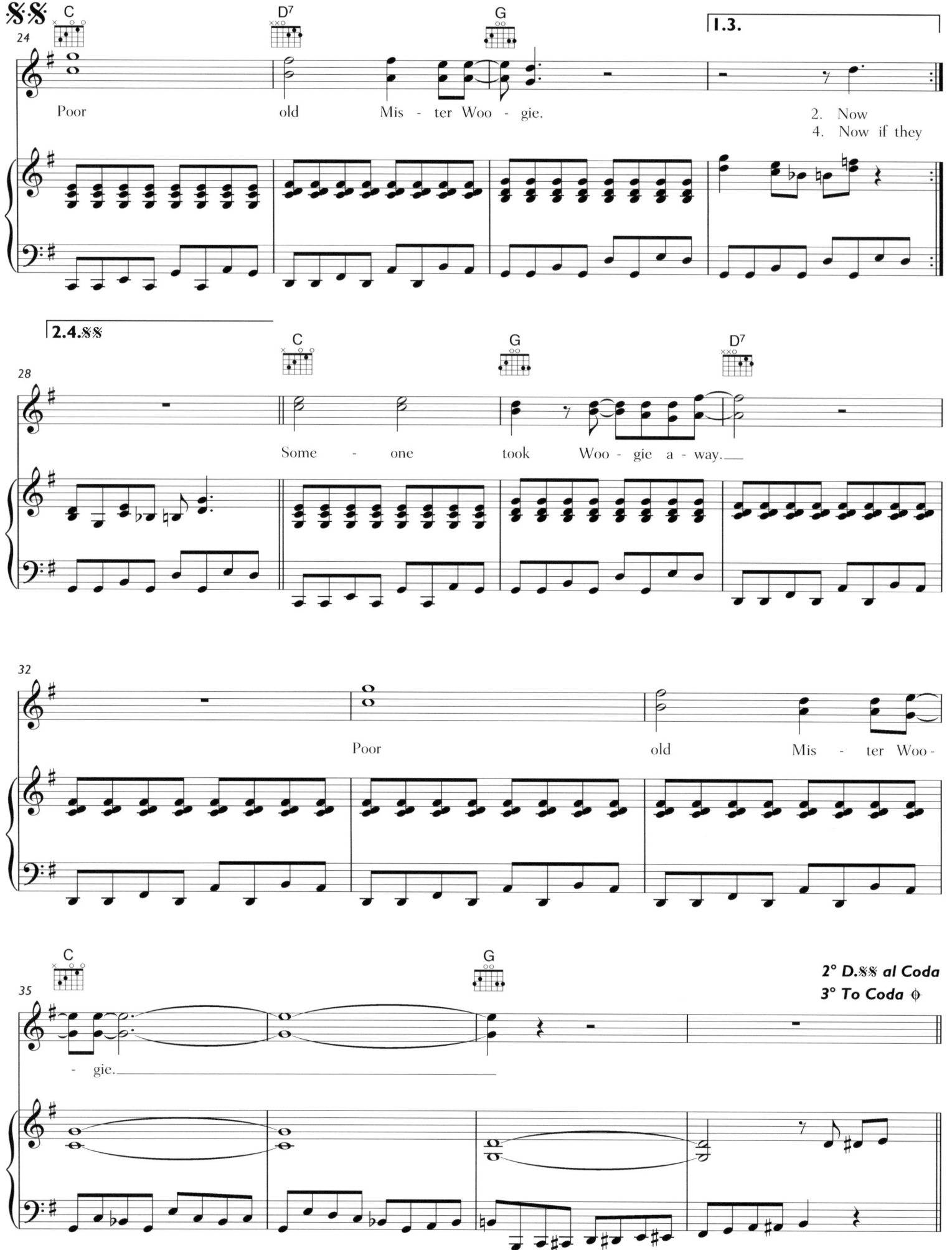

RABBIT
Words and Music by Charles Hodges and David Peacock

© 1979 Snout Music Ltd

THE SIDEBOARD SONG
Words and Music by Charles Hodges and David Peacock

© 1979 Snout Music Ltd

THAT OLD PIANO
Words and Music by Charles Hodges and David Peacock

© 1982 Snout Music Ltd

THAT'S WHAT I LIKE
Words and Music by Charles Hodges and David Peacock

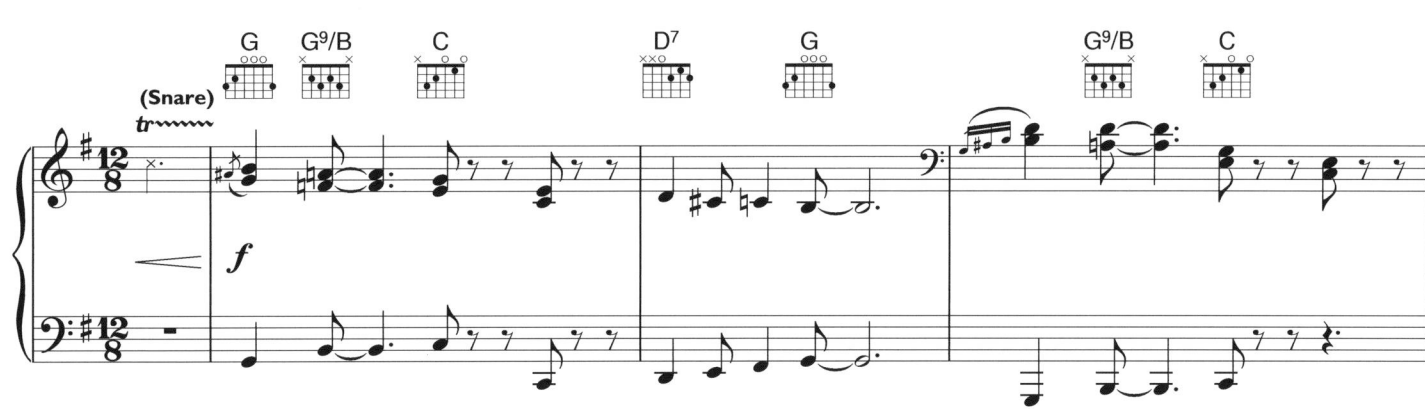

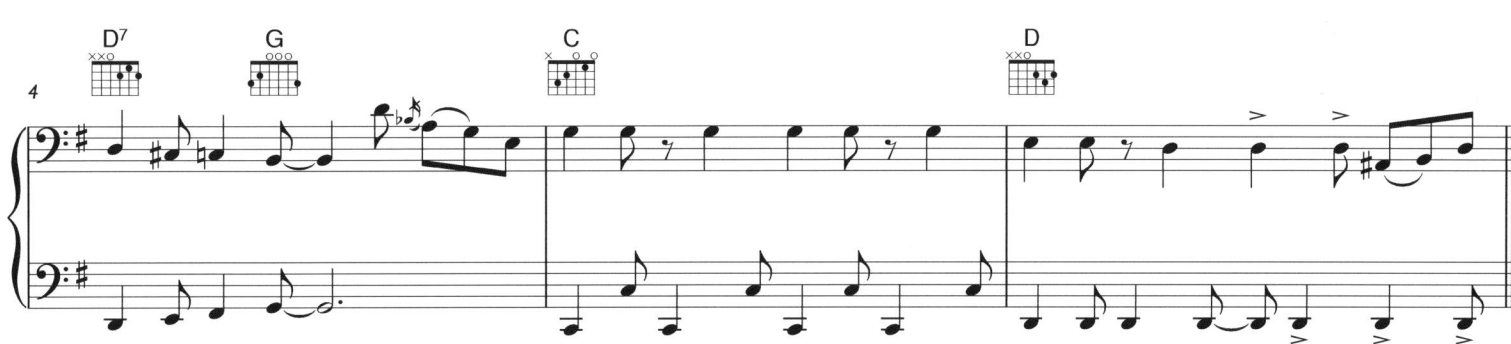

1. Cheese and on-ion sand-wich-es and Der-by chin-a-ware, fid-dles and jigs, and Woog-ie me dog, me
2. Pie and mash 'n li-quor and walking a-bout in the rain, Wil-li-am books, com-i-cal looks, pi-
3. Lit-tle pubs out in the country, mother of pearl and Barnet fair, the sound of a banjo, bar-ber shop singing and
4. Bubble and squeak and jum-ble sales, Little Richard and Jer-ry Lee, bon-fire nights, South-end lights and

© 1982 Snout Music Ltd

G G9/B C
16
old wood - en wheels and a bowl of eels.
foun - tain pens and the Beano and Dandy.
Shir - ley Mac - Laine_ and Petti - coat Lane.
fish - ing rods, frogs_ and Spurs are winning.
1, 3.
D7 G G9/B C D7 G
18
That's what I like,_
that's what I like._
2.
D7 G C D
that's what I like._

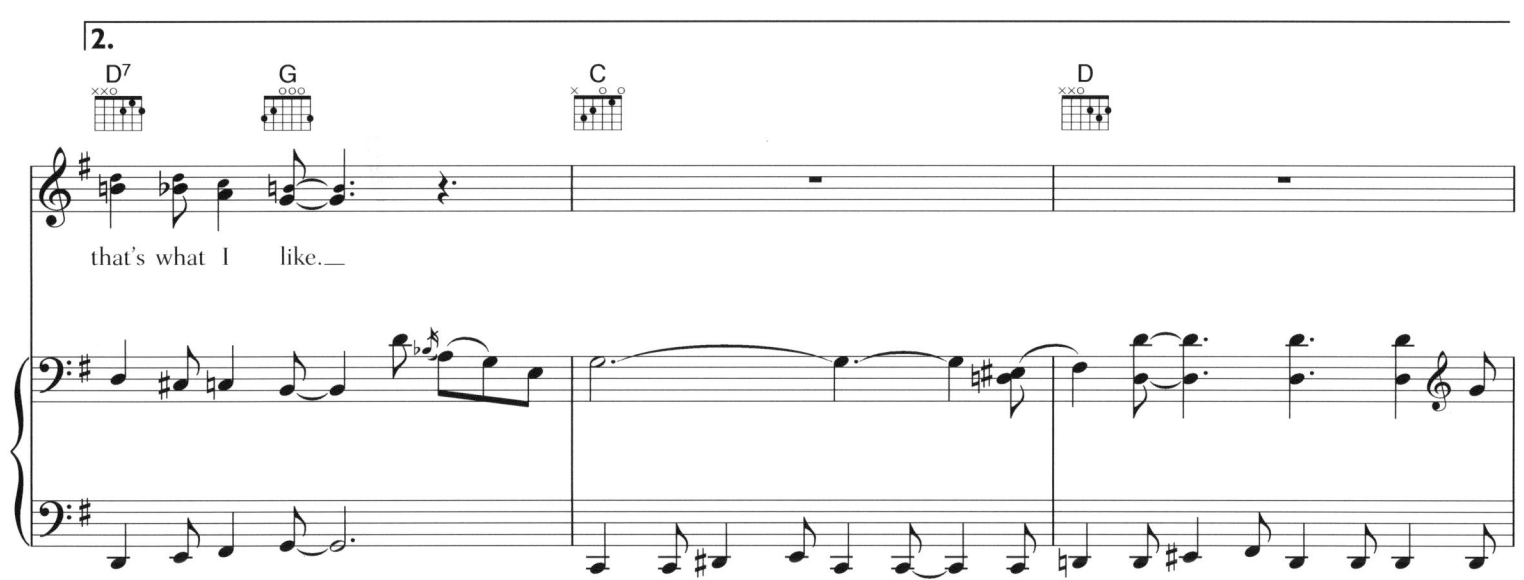

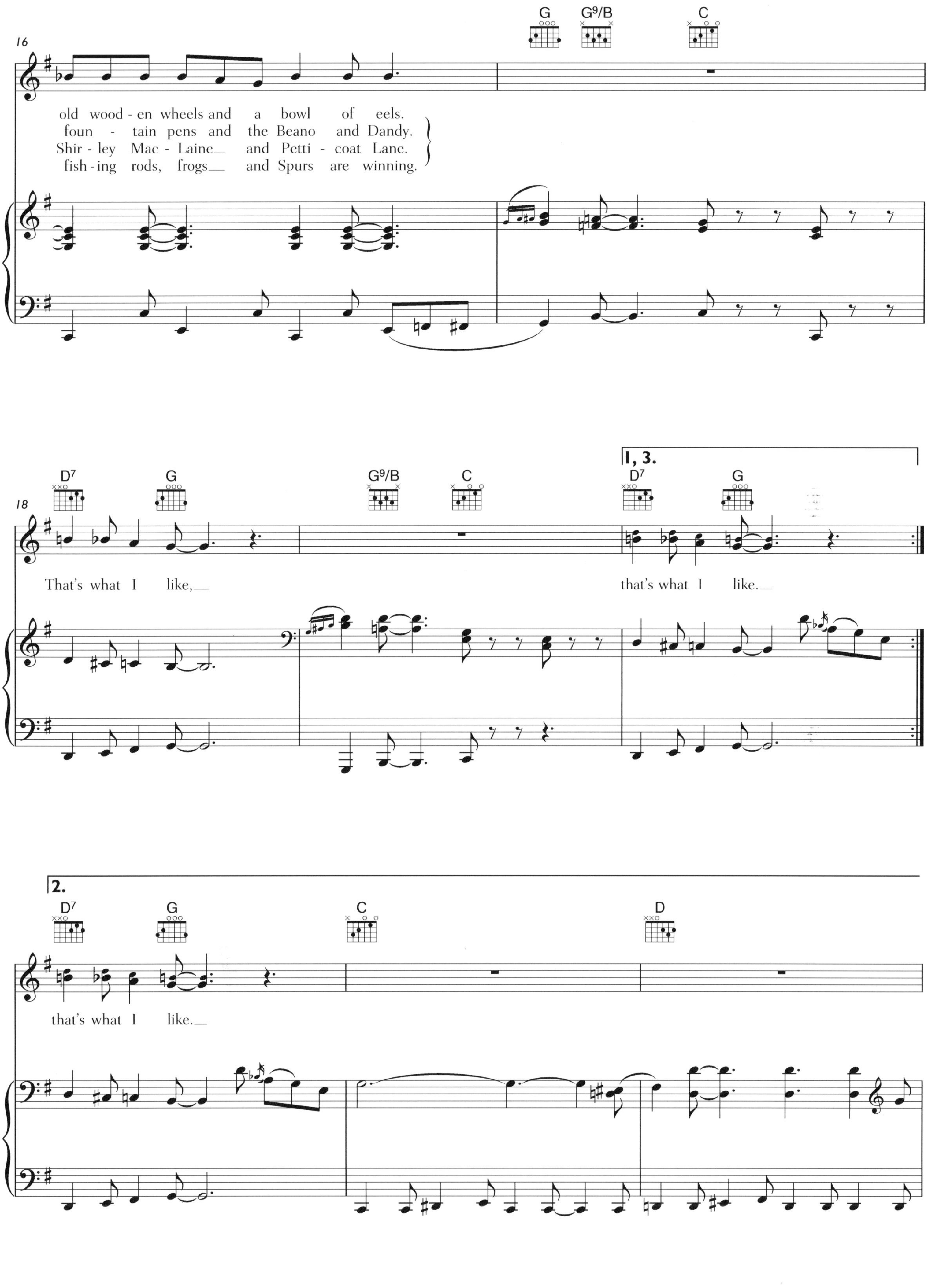

94

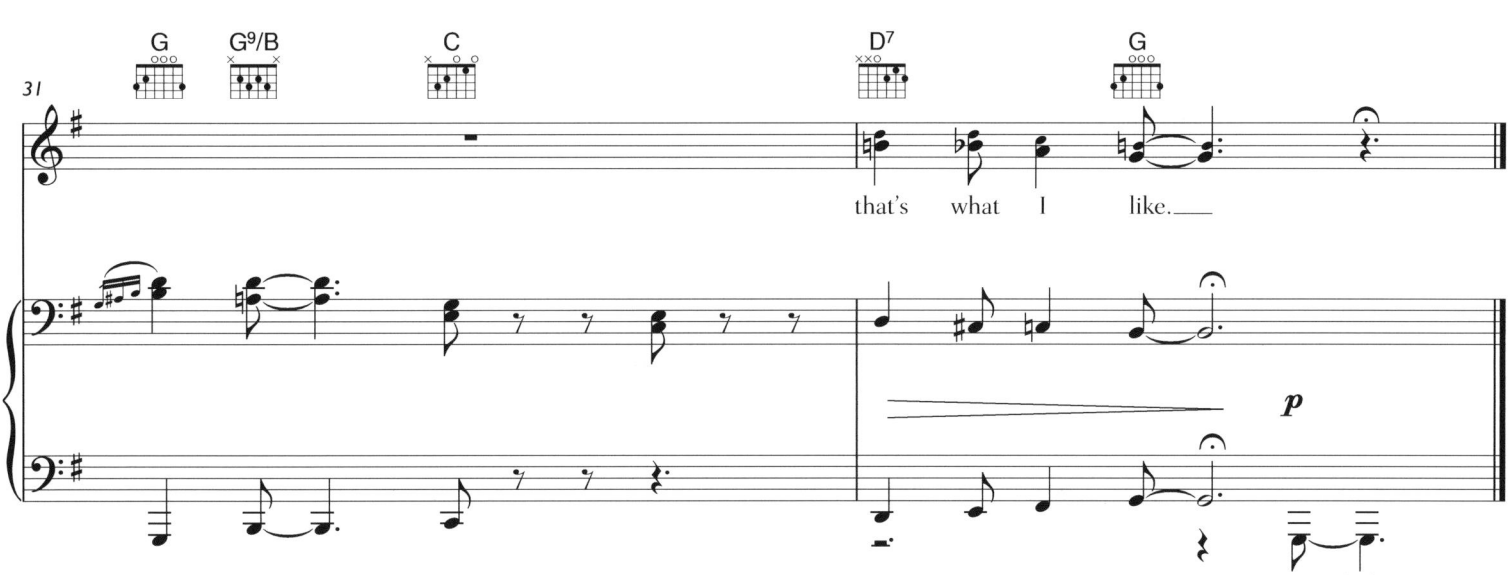

WISH I COULD WRITE A LOVE SONG
Words and Music by Charles Hodges and David Peacock

© 1982 Snout Music Ltd

WALLOP
Words and Music by Charles Hodges and David Peacock

© 1981 Snout Music Ltd